FOOD INVENTORS

by
Rebecca Phillips-Bartlett

Minneapolis, Minnesota

Credits

All images are courtesy of Shutterstock.com, unless otherwise specified. With thanks to Getty Images, Thinkstock Photo, and iStockphoto.

Recurring images – Andrew Rybalko, cosmaa, andromina, P-fotography, Mark Rademaker. Cover – Andrew Rybalko, dimair, Happy Oksana, Pogorelova Olga, WinWin artlab, cosmaa, andromina, P-fotography. 2–3 – VectorShow. 4–5 – kornnphoto, Standret, dimair, jjshaw14. 6–7 – Wikimedia Commons/Public Domain, VectorShow, TeraVector, AlenKadr, William C. Minor. 8–9 – Wikimedia Commons/Public Domain, Happy Oksana, Evgeny Karandaev, BlueRingMedia, GoodStudio, NIKCOA. 10–11 – Animalparty, stockcreations, Emil Timplaru, kaisorn. 12–13 – Pogorelova Olga, WinWin artlab, Pixel-Shot, Navakun Suwantragu, Tilden76. 14–15 –Scewing, serazetdinov, Kovaleva_Ka. 16–17 – Timmary, Victoria Sergeeva. 18–19 – dimair, Iconic Bestiary, Farah Sadikhova, Dzha33. 20–21 – Dcoetzee, GifTagger, wavebreakmedia, wowomnom, Sudowoodo, Magicleaf. 22–23 –Africa Studio, GoodStudio, WinWin artlab, Torychemistry, NIKCOA.

Library of Congress Cataloging-in-Publication Data

Names: Phillips-Bartlett, Rebecca, 1999- author.
Title: Food inventors / by Rebecca Phillips-Bartlett.
Description: Minneapolis, Minnesota : Bearport Publishing Company, [2024] | Series: Brilliant people, big ideas | Includes index.
Identifiers: LCCN 2023030997 (print) | LCCN 2023030998 (ebook) | ISBN 9798889163565 (hardcover) | ISBN 9798889163619 (paperback) | ISBN 9798889163657 (ebook)
Subjects: LCSH: Food engineers--Biography--Juvenile literature. | Food science--Juvenile literature. | Food industry and trade--Technological innovations--Juvenile literature.
Classification: LCC TP369.5 .P45 2024 (print) | LCC TP369.5 (ebook) | DDC 664.0092--dc23/eng/20230717
LC record available at https://lccn.loc.gov/2023030997
LC ebook record available at https://lccn.loc.gov/2023030998

© 2024 BookLife Publishing
This edition is published by arrangement with BookLife Publishing.

North American adaptations © 2024 Bearport Publishing Company. All rights reserved. No part of this publication may be reproduced in whole or in part, stored in any retrieval system, or transmitted in any form or by any means, electronic, mechanical, photocopying, recording, or otherwise, without written permission from the publisher.

For more information, write to Bearport Publishing, 5357 Penn Avenue South, Minneapolis, MN 55419.

Contents

Big Ideas 4
Nicolas Appert 6
James Mease 8
Nancy Johnson 10
William Morrison 12
George Washington Carver 14
Otto Frederick Rohwedder 16
Rose Totino 18
The Hall of Fame 20
All You Need Is an Idea! 22
Glossary 24
Index 24

Big Ideas

What is your favorite food? Do you know the first person to make this tasty treat or meal?

From yummy frozen pizzas to colorful cotton candy, who do we have to thank for our favorite food **inventions**? These chefs, scientists, and inventors were **brilliant** people with big ideas!

Let's find out which foods come from amazing inventions!

Nicolas Appert

My food keeps going bad! How can I make it last longer?

1749–1841

Food Canning

James Mease

1771–1846

"I do not have the right **ingredients** to make ketchup. I wonder what else I could use...."

Tomato Ketchup

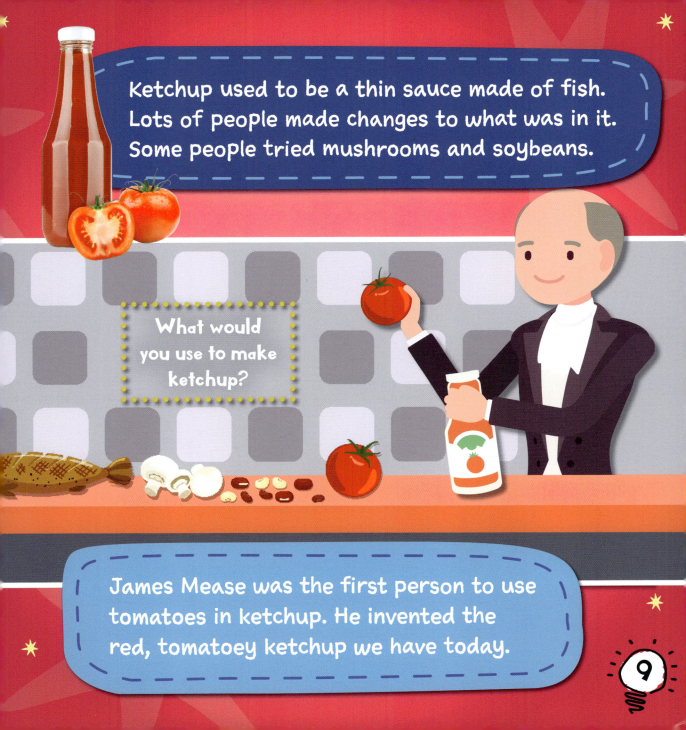

Before Nancy Johnson, ice cream was very difficult to make. She invented an ice cream maker that let more people easily make the cold treat at home.

What do you think is the best ice cream flavor?

Nancy's **machine** worked just like ice cream makers today. It made cream very cold and mixed it until it was smooth.

William Morrison

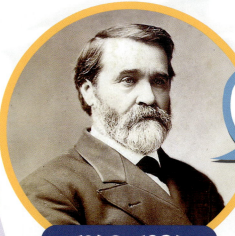

I am a dentist. Still, I want to make a sweet treat.

1860–1926

Cotton Candy

Cotton candy is just sugar and air. A machine melts the sugar and stretches it into long, thin pieces. Then, the sugar can be wrapped around a stick.

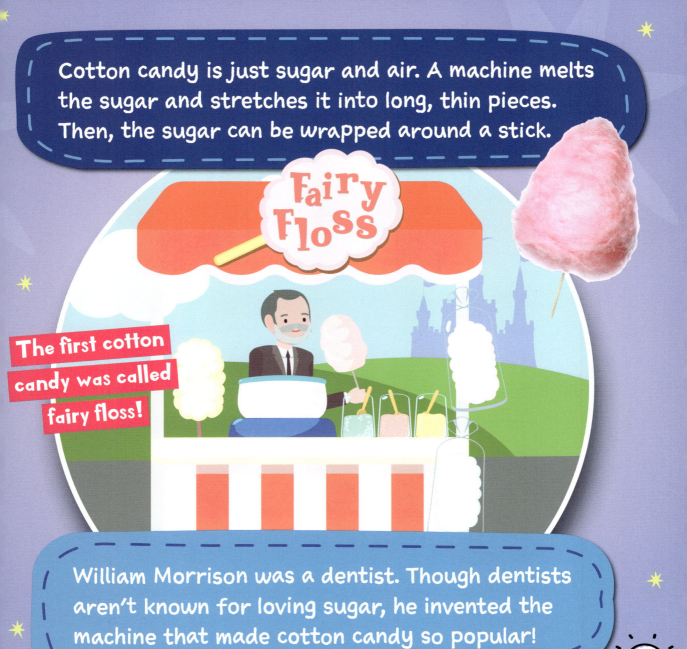

The first cotton candy was called fairy floss!

William Morrison was a dentist. Though dentists aren't known for loving sugar, he invented the machine that made cotton candy so popular!

George Washington Carver

How can I help farmers?

1864–1943

Peanut Recipes

George Washington Carver saw many farmers struggling. Things weren't growing well. George found that if you mix up the things you plant, the **soil** is healthier. Everything grows better.

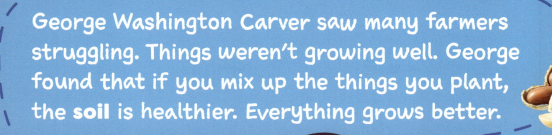

George Washington Carver was the first Black American to have a **monument** built to remember him.

He told people to plant peanuts to help their cotton. It worked, but then farmers had more peanuts than they needed. So, George came up with new **recipes** to use the peanuts!

Otto Frederick Rohwedder

1880–1960

Who needs the hassle of cutting their own bread? I have an idea....

Sliced Bread

People used to buy whole loaves of bread. They had to slice the bread themselves. Then, Otto Frederick Rohwedder invented the first bread-slicing machine.

People now often call a great new idea the best thing since sliced bread!

Otto's first plans burned in a fire. He faced many other **challenges** along the way. But now, people buy sliced bread every day!

Rose Totino

1915–1994

"Frozen pizza tastes so bad. Imagine if it was actually yummy...."

Tasty Frozen Pizza

Rose Totino owned a restaurant with her husband. They sold pizza to-go. But her customers wanted more. The Totinos figured out how to freeze pizzas so more people could enjoy fresh pies at home.

Rose Totino was the first woman in the Frozen Food Hall of Fame!

Earlier frozen pizzas tasted terrible! The Totinos made the first ones that actually tasted good.

The Hall of Fame

Here are some more brilliant people who deserve a place in our food hall of fame.

John Montagu, the Fourth Earl of Sandwich

Some people think John Montagu invented sandwiches. He probably didn't come up with the idea, but the Earl of Sandwich did give the food its name!

Alfred Cralle

After seeing people struggling to serve ice cream, Alfred Cralle invented the ice cream scoop!

Eco-Friendly Eaters

Some people are thinking of ways to help the planet with food. Scientists are inventing water bottles that you can eat!

All You Need Is an Idea!

From tasty frozen pizzas to sliced bread, many of our favorite foods wouldn't be the same without brilliant people.

Some of these inventors came up with yummy new ideas. Others looked at food that already existed and tried to make it even better. Either way, we are grateful that they did!

What could you invent to change the world of food?

Glossary

brilliant extremely smart

challenges things that are hard to do or deal with

ingredients the different foods that are used to make something

inventions new things that have been made to solve problems

machine a thing with moving parts used to do work

monument something built to remember a person or an event

recipes lists of steps for making food

soil dirt or earth in which plants grow

Index

canned foods 6–7
cotton candy 5, 12–13
frozen pizzas 5, 18–19, 22
ice cream makers 10–11
ice cream scoops 21
jars 7
peanuts 14–15
sandwiches 20
sliced bread 16–17, 22
tomato ketchup 8–9